5 Steps to Animal Communication

Listening to Your Animals Made Easy

Cindy Myers

©2016 Cynthia Myers

Dedication

This book is dedicated to all my animal companions both living and those that have crossed over. Each one has helped me develop my intuition. Their life lessons have enhanced my life. Rusty, Fawkes, Harper, Wiley, Moose, Tesla, Jamilah, Sargon, Dulcinea, Miss Marple, and all the rest of my wonderful herd of creatures deserve my heartfelt gratitude. I'm incredibly fortunate to have three of the most wonderful sisters. Sally, Hannah and Ilene have been supportive and terrific as I live such an out of the box life. And thanks to all my great and wonderful friends especially; Alison who is my encourager; Ann is my alpaca buddy through good times and bad; and Elissa, who shared Minnie with me as I honed my craft. And special note of thanks to Vee and Sam for proofreading this book.

Note from the Author

It is my life's mission to help us humans become better listeners. Animals are the best teachers in helping us learn to listen beyond our words. Our society is in desperate need of us working on our listening skills. We are becoming a society of emoticons, detached from each other, and when connecting to each other, it is via mobile phones and devices. We are losing the skill and art of listening to each other which goes beyond the superficiality of short hand texts. Animals are the perfect teachers in educating us on the value and wonderment of connecting with each other using such an intimate and special intuitive way. My hope is that this book opens to others these amazing and life altering intuitively connected moments and experiences.

5 Steps to Animal Communication

Introduction: Why Animal Listener?

Many years ago, I worked as an engineer at a Naval base. I was a first-line supervisor there for many years. I've always been a good listener, and people would come to me often, telling me their concerns, issues, and other matters whether it was good or bad news. I made it a point to have an open-door policy.

One day, all the supervisors were called into a meeting with the base's captain. He wanted to go over a recent survey all employees had taken. The results showed that communication and morale were the employees' main concerns. I wasn't surprised because employees regularly expressed to me their dissatisfaction and angst. The captain lectured us that supervisors needed to do a better job of communicating to all what was going on at the base. However, since I had already been talking with the people, I knew that wasn't their issue. The real issue was the fact that employees' concerns weren't being heard and listened to. It was a one-way conversation with plenty of talking to people but no listening in return.

I took this as an opportunity to promote the listening piece of having a conversation. I said to my colleagues, "Conversation has two elements. One element is the talking piece, which we can always strive to do better and become more effective at doing. However, the other element entails the '*listening*' piece." Before I could elaborate on what I meant, the captain slammed his hand on the conference table and stated, "You're *right*! So when you are talking to your folks, make sure they are listening to *you*!" I sat there stunned and not sure what to say, and it didn't matter because he took the conversation over and went on talking.

This really happened, and although I always get a laugh at the absurdity and irony of this story, not listening really is something we are all guilty of to some degree, especially where our animals are concerned.

When I start my Animal Communication course, I like to ask what people hope to get out of the class. Many say they want to be able to talk to their animals better. Or, "I want to be able to talk to my pet." In other words, the expectation and hope is that our animals will be able to listen to us and they will understand what we are saying to them. The word *listening* is rarely used.

I've been called an "alpaca whisperer" and an "animal whisperer," but I prefer to call myself an Animal Listener.

What's the difference? To me, there is a big difference. Most people who talk about being a whisperer are talking to the animal with the expectation that the animal will listen better because of how we talk to it. *Whisper* after all means talking just in a low volume. *Listening* means you are not talking at all. You are listening to the animal instead of talking to it. In other words, listeners are open to receiving instead of always doing the sending.

Consider the differences between the phrases *talking at, talking to*, and t*alking with* someone. Which one do you think is most effective? Which one would you prefer if someone wanted to have a conversation with you? Would you prefer to be talked at? Talked to? Or, talked with?

My definition of "*talking at*" someone is that the speaker has all the answers, and he or she is talking to the other from a position of superiority. Perhaps that is just a negative perspective but even in a positive situation, you may still get talked at, for instance, during a church sermon. You may be told a positive message, but the information is only being sent out to be received. It is one direction. It doesn't usually allow for information coming back.

Being talked to reminds me of children being scolded. They will get a good talking to over their behavior. It implies a one-way direction, and that is usually how it goes.

Talking *with* someone is more welcoming a phrase than talking to and talking at, but it also encourages a dialogue and two-way communication that includes both talking and listening on the part of all participants.

Depending on the setting and reason, all these methods are ways of communicating. Communicating *with* your animal will provide you both with a deeper bond and I believe that is true in any relationship including ones we have with humans.

My first real paying career was working as an engineer, and my first project involved working on radars. It wasn't until years later and my intuitive work was in full swing that it made sense why I was drawn to radar work. After all, that is pretty much what I do now as an animal communicator and intuitive energy worker. I am a human radar. I send out signals, receive them, and then interpret those signals into useful information. When we communicate, it is the same. We send out verbal information, and we hope someone receives it and they are able to interpret it accurately.

Having your communication accurately heard is not always easy. Remember that telephone game where one person starts and whispers a phrase in the ear of someone then that person who received the whisper, does the same to someone else? Each person continues whispering what he or she hears to the next person until the message comes back to the original person who started the game. When the original person hears that final whisper, it is, more often than not, totally different than what he or she originally whispered.

There are ways of being an effective speaker, but no matter how good you are at providing the perfect words, if the person you're communicating with isn't good at listening, then your words will get jumbled up and created into a new meaning. Even when we take classes on effective communication, much of the time is spent on how to say things using assertive phrasing, but not a lot of time is spent on active listening and building those skills. And that is what we humans need most of all. Our listening skills are getting weaker and weaker. We communicate now in short-hand, mobile friendly, and emoticon language.

Our language, especially the English language, is not always accurately interpreted. Our vocabulary is pretty limiting if you think about it. Take the word "*love*" for example. We can love romantically, we can love our children, we can love our pets, we can love chocolate chip cookies. Each type is different in meaning, and yet we use the same word for all those meanings.

With animals, their verbal vocabulary is even more limiting. Consider a dog. How many sounds does it make for verbal communication? There are growls: the play growl, the growl that means business, and the I'm warning you off growl. There is a high-pitch play bark that signifies excitement to see someone come home. There is a deeper bark that is again a warning. There is also a ferocious bark that is used in the midst of fighting. There are yelps of pain, whimpers, and whines but when compared to our verbal language, a dog's verbal vocabulary is minimal. The same is true for most animals.

Animals may not have much of a verbal language. However, they use other means to communicate with others more effectively than us humans. They use body language, scent, hearing, and their intuitive ways more than we do. How do many animals greet one another? They sniff each others' rear ends. Could you imagine that being the acceptable and normal way we greet one another? But why do they greet that way instead of barking or using other verbal language? Scent gives them a lot of information about the other animal. But even before they greet each other and sniff tushes, they have already given each other permission to do so using their body language. Ear position, tail and eyes all provide each animal a great deal of information prior to that initial sniff.

Humans also use body language; however, we are typically not very conscious of any of these other communication cues. We don't usually recognize it amongst ourselves, and we tend to blow right past it when animals are using their bodies to communicate to us. And they really believe we are not very capable at all of understanding their intuitive language. However, when you do use some basic simple techniques like in this book, you will find animals respond to you in such a special way. They finally feel heard.

Think about how good it feels when you finally feel heard. After all, isn't that something that we all basically desire?

I worked with a small dog who was using very aggressive means of communicating her wish to be left alone. She felt very vulnerable and was in a state of fear and even with her beloved owners, she was too afraid to let them near her. So to get them to understand that was her desire, she would snarl, bare her teeth, and snap if they ignored her and came too close.

I was asked to come and see if I could assist in modifying her behavior. As I observed her, she gave off signals before the snarling and snapping stage that her owners didn't recognize. I taught them what to look for in her body language so they could listen better to their dog and prevent her snapping before it happened. When I sat on the floor with her and allowed her to come to me in a quiet fashion, offering a lot of positive reinforcement with tasty treats, she came out of her shell. If she didn't want it, I ignored her and turned my back on her. Soon she showed signs that she wanted to engage with me, using eye contact, wags of her tail, and sitting when I asked. She got to choose her behavior, and if she showed any sign of feeling vulnerable and scared, I'd respond by giving her space and moving my body away from her. She felt heard. She trusted me in two quick sessions of working with her.

When we listen to our animals, we build trust. I use the metaphor of a bank account when describing relationships. We want to have a healthy relationship account, and to get that healthy relationship account, we have to put in a lot of positive experiences. With animals, it can be treats, playing with favorites toys, or petting. Perhaps they love being brushed or going for walks. Anything that they like that they can be rewarded for can build up that account.

I don't reward behaviors I don't want. I try to ignore those. Or, if need be, I'll put one of us in a timeout. If one of my alpacas spits at me when we are having treats, game over. My treats and I go away. Or I will work with that one to get them to do what I want. Perhaps I take a step back, and I know how to use body language so they are less likely to spit. I look for ways to set them up for success and earn rewards. But I will not reward bad behavior. I will wait, walk away, and then come back and set them up so they can experience the difference.

I like clicker training because I can communicate with the animal effectively. I reward what moment, behavior, and body language they are doing that I like. With my spitty alpaca, I will click her when she takes a step back. I use both her body and my body language to get her to take the step back and she will get a click. I understand her body language well enough to know that feeding her treats with her head pointing downward is teaching her not to spit. Alpacas most often spit with their heads tilted with their chins pointing to the sky. If I can lure them into a body position with their head pointed downward, it tells them they are not in the spitting position and it is way more rare that they spit. It takes only a few consecutive clicks, and they move to that position on their own. We have communicated with each other effectively without speaking a word.

Clicker training is one way of communicating and a great tool, however it is based on behavior modification and not intuitive communication. When I work with people to assist them with pet behavioral issues, I help to modify the undesirable behavior, and I also work with the owners to find out what behaviors they *do* want their pets to exhibit. Just removing the energy that created the undesirable behavior isn't enough. The pet will default out of habit to the old behavior even if we have removed the trapped emotions that created it originally. We need to let the animal know what the desirable behavior is and reward them heavily to establish the behavior.

When dealing with a fearful animal, listening to their body language and taking a step away, turning sideways so you are in a less aggressive stance, and lowering eyes so you're not looking at them directly, will communicate to them you are respecting their emotional state. Letting them have space can also be additions to the account. Doing things that are not positive yet necessary, will take away from the account. Maybe they don't like their nails trimmed, but that is important to do for their well-being so we must do it. However, it can deplete the trust bank account. If we have a nice big account, it typically doesn't affect the relationship. Animals get over it very fast.   But if you don't have a big relationship account or you have just rescued an animal and they have come from a fearful place where they have had negative experiences with humans, your account is low or in the red. Doing some of these techniques I will describe in this book, will help build that bank account even if, and most importantly, you start the relationship with a new pet and a negative bank account.

The great news about these techniques is that they are easy to learn. Some are automatic like the techniques in the chapter on breathing (beginning on page 11). Using them with intention and consciousness is what matters. Our animals actually listen to us a great deal of the time. We may not listen to them, but they are listening to us. When you start using these techniques, you will notice a difference. Our animals show their appreciation for being heard in so many wonderful ways.

One last story before we get into the real substance (I love telling stories about my animal experiences!). I had an alpaca come to my farm. This alpaca had been boarded at the same farm I was boarding my alpacas before I moved my herd and me to Oregon. She was a cranky, spitty alpaca. If someone (even another alpaca), looked at her, she would turn them green with her noxious smelling spit. No animal had ever turned me more green, and it was disgusting! When her owners moved to Oregon and needed a temporary place to board her while they built their home, they asked me if I'd keep her along with their animals. I was eager for the income but a part of me was dreading having this alpaca on my farm and having to take care of her. But I decided, it would be fine.

She came with her herd mates, and she still spat as I walked too close to her. But one day not long after she arrived, as I walked past her, I saw the look in her eyes as she did a little puff spit at me. She had such a look of fear and panic in her eyes. That fearful look climbed right into my heart, and I felt such compassion for her. I knew I could work with fear.

Working with an animal that is just plain cantankerous is hard, but I can more easily work with fear-based behavior. It takes patience and looking for ways to build that bank account. I reached out with my mind and welcomed her. I truly welcomed her from my heart and told her she was safe at my farm.

Not long after I noticed this alpaca's fearful state, I was filling up water buckets. She came close to me and raised her front leg. I believed she was asking to get squirted with the hose. I sprayed her chest and legs. She stayed there and then even stepped closer to me to enjoy the hose. I wanted to fill up my bank account with her. I was thrilled that I found something she wanted from me. I pulled the hose away to fill the water bucket. I wanted to see what this alpaca would do when the water stopped spraying her. Sure enough, she raised her leg to ask for the hose. I sprayed her again. We did this over and over. I had her asking and was able to respond. She knew I was listening to her and giving her what she wanted. (It is more effective to do repetitive rewards than one giant jackpot. Each quick reward is a deposit. One big reward is the same as a small amount of a treat. Therefore, providing lots of little rewards adds more into your account than one big one).

The hose was a "Ka-Ching" opportunity! After that, she was my friend. She hung out with me all the time. She slowly trusted me enough to take carrots and treats from my hand. If someone else was visiting, she'd stand near us and act like she was enjoying the conversation. Her owner came to the farm to visit his animals. We were chatting along the fence line and this alpaca came over and stood next to us calm as could be. He asked who this alpaca was? I said, "She is yours." He said, "No way!" She learned to take treats from us and discovered a real love of carrots, and she adores children. She has since become one of his farm favorites.

I hope learning the techniques in this book will help you build the accounts with your animal companions and bring you much joy and deep connections. My intuitive work with animals has been life enhancing and has made me a better human.

Step 1: Breathing in Fours

Owning an alpaca farm makes life interesting. You never know what each day or even each moment will bring. One evening, I was walking out to my barn area to begin my evening chores when I noticed Miss Marple, one of my alpacas, laying on her side. Alpacas can lay on their side, and that is not abnormal; however, there was something about it that made me stop and watch her for a moment. I had a little inkling that maybe something wasn't right. Why did I think that? Was it just intuition? Perhaps some of it was my intuitive connection with Miss Marple. But, I also know extremely well what each of my animals normal behavior is like. I had never recalled Miss Marple laying on her side at that time of the evening. She would earlier in the day when the sun was out and warm. Alpacas will point their bellies, where they have less fiber, towards the sun. Yet this evening, the sun was setting in the horizon and she was pointing her belly towards the east. I have also never seen her lay down in that particular spot. Alpacas have their favorite resting places, and that was not one of them. I had clues that something was maybe amiss, but I also thought perhaps she was just tired. So I went out to check on her, and she popped right up. I thought I was just being a worrier. I went about my business but when I looked back at Miss Marple a short time later, she was laying back down on her side. That too is very unusual behavior. Once they get up, they rarely lay back down like that.

I walked over to her again. She popped right back up. Herd animals tend to want to hide the fact they are not feeling well. The weakest are prone to being the ones attacked by predators so it is a pretty hard-wired instinct to hide the fact they don't feel well. I decided she needed to be watched more closely. I continued with our evening feeding routine, and as I put out their favorite pellets, I observed that Miss Marple didn't go to eat like the rest. That is really unusual behavior. She loves her pellets and is always first to a bowl. That was when I *knew* she didn't feel well.

I decided I'd better catch Miss Marple, do some investigation on what might be wrong, begin any treatments if necessary, and call my vet. He always wants a temperature taken, so I knew to try to get that before calling. Miss Marple is perhaps the smartest alpaca in my herd. She is exceptionally bright, and she also just recently had a baby so given those two facts and her not feeling well, she picked up that I was trying to catch her. She was having none of that. She would not enter the catch pen where it is easier to hold her by putting on a halter. I tried everything to get her into the catching area. It is nearly impossible to catch an alpaca in spacious open fields. They are faster than I am and have great moves. I wasn't coming close to being able to catch her. I was getting more anxious and worried about her though because every time I stopped one of my tricks to get her in the catch pen, she'd lay down. Something was wrong, and I really needed to catch her to assess what was up.

After at least 10 minutes of trying every trick I knew to get an alpaca into a catch pen, I just stopped and said to myself, "What am I doing? Why don't I just talk to her intuitively." So I stopped and took several deep breaths. My breathing was shallow due to anxiety and running about. I was very worried by this point. I slowed down my breathing, reached out to her with my mind, and told her that I really needed to catch her to see if I could help her feel better. Would she please let me take a step closer to her?

I received the reply "yes" that I could take one step closer. I took the one step. I took another deep breath and asked again, "May I please take a step closer?" I received the yes reply again. I repeated this process until I was standing by her side. I asked her, "May I please place my hand on your neck?" She was tentative, but I got a yes to my question. I gently reached up and placed my hand high on her neck which allows me to hold her firmly without her having leverage to break free. I held her and was able to put her halter on as quietly as could be in the wide open pasture. And, I was able to gain her trust and connect with her because I stopped acting like a predator and remembered to breathe and talk to her in the language she understood and in a way she could hear it.

Every time I communicate with an animal or do my intuitive energy work, I begin with deep breaths. It is absolutely the most important thing you can do to connect with an animal. Our animals are listening to us all the time. If we are stressed, worried, or upset, we don't breathe fully. Even if we are not in that negative emotional state, we tend not to breathe very fully. But the more stressed out we are, the shallower our breath. Animals are very tuned into that. If you are walking your dog and you are anxious, your anxiety radiates right through the lead line. Your dog will become tense and be more vigilant and reactive if you are anxious while holding the lead. But if you take deep breaths and can calm yourself, that too will be conveyed through the lead line, and if they are listening, they will pick that up.

I do an exercise with my classes that involves a lead rope. I have a student hold the lead as if they were the animal. I first have them tense up as if they are really anxious. I have them breathe shallowly and tighten all their muscles. They are gripping the lead as tight as they can with their eyes closed tightly. I ask them to tell me to stop when they feel my hand moving up the lead line towards their hand. Invariably I get to about 6 inches from their hand when they tell me to stop. This is the distance between my hand and at which they feel my presence on the lead rope. I have them relax. I ask them to take several deep, full breaths. I have them unlock their knees and relax as best they can, and we repeat the exercise. They often tell me they feel my hand at least a foot or two further away down the lead rope. When we are calm and breathing, we can hear each other much better.

When your dog is anxious, it will take longer for them to hear your directions and cues using the lead than if they are calm. If you are both anxious, then you both will take longer to hear each other. That results in your arm being yanked hard. By the time our eyes see something and process that we need to react, the dog is already moving and pulling on the leash. But if we are feeling it and tuned into them, we can sense the tension, and if we are really listening to them, we can correct and be ready before they are pulling our arm out of its socket.

When I walk my dog Wiley, I sometimes close my eyes for a few moments and just feel the line. I can tell when he moves ever so slightly. If he picks up a scent he wants to check out, I can feel the leash move to one direction or the other, or if he sees a squirrel perhaps, I can feel the tension in the line. I can more easily correct him back to the heeling position and walk at our pace with a mere tap on the lead when we are both listening. I can also feel it through the lead line faster than my eyes can see what he is doing.

In other words, listening to the lead line allows me to prevent the undesirable behavior before it gets any momentum. I know how far I need my hand down on the line depending on what his excitement and anxiety level is so that he can hear me and I can correct things before they become big corrections. When we are in sync with each other, it is such a beautiful connection. I literally can tap the lead with my pinky finger, and he moves accordingly to my gentle and quiet lead direction. It is the lightest touch to the line, yet he hears it and responds. Taking walks with that level of communication and connection deepens our bond with each other.

To be that connected and in tune with your animal, you must breathe. Sounds simple, and it really is. I can tell you, however, that we all forget to do so. And if we don't fully breathe, it makes it so much harder if not impossible to have that connection. In my classes, I am forever reminding my students, "Are you breathing?" And the most common reply is, "No, I forgot!"

Just like we need to breathe and be calm to hear what is going on with the lead line, as we develop our intuition, we also need to practice our breathing. I believe our intuition is communicating to us all the time. We just aren't listening to it. We aren't listening to it because our minds are so busy with the work meeting, the grocery list, the kids activities, the fight we had with someone, and so on. We are a society that is in our heads. If we aren't in our heads, we are on our cell phones reading texts and emails, and thinking about replying to those messages. We are the busiest culture. One of the most common reasons why people tell me they "can't" communicate with animals is because they can't quiet and still their minds to listen.

Training yourself to breathe will help you calm all that mind clutter. A very simple technique I start people with is what I call "breathing in fours." If you can count to four, you can do this exercise. Take a full, deep breath while counting to four as you do so. Go as slowly as you can but keep inflating your lungs so that they are fully inflated when you get to four. Then hold your breath for another count of four. Then exhale, emptying your lungs slowly on another count of four. Keep your lungs empty for a count of four, and then repeat the full process four times.

Doing this very simple exercise before you work with an animal will help you connect much more deeply with them and will help calm both of you. If you are taking your pet to the vet and they are anxious, do this exercise and it will help calm them. If you are in a stressful meeting, you can do this exercise very quietly and it will help reduce your stress and help your mind stay clear and focused. What is interesting is that others often will begin taking their own fuller breaths intuitively when they are near someone doing so. Think of how contagious yawns are! This simple breathing technique is good for your own health and well-being, and it is the basic first step in connecting with any animal. They do respond to calm individuals.

The more you practice this simple breathing technique, the more second nature it will become. You want taking several deep breaths whenever you work with your animals to be a fairly automatic habit, and even more importantly, you should do it every time you feel stressed. When I was a kid and took piano lessons, we always warmed up our hands by doing scales. Think of the breathing in fours as like doing piano scales to help quiet your mind. It prepares your body to receive intuitive connections, and it indicates to your pet that you want to connect with them.

This technique helps when connecting with people, too. If I find I'm having a hard time connecting with an animal or person, I take more deep breaths. Even when I work at a distance where the animal or person is in a different city or locale than me, I always begin with my deep-breathing exercises.

I was at an alpaca show. One of the events is called "get of sire." Owners take three offspring of a male-stud alpaca. Each owner needs two other people to help show all three since it is not easy to handle one, let alone three. I was asked if I'd help take one of the young alpacas into the show ring with his owner. I was happy to do so. The little male that I had was very skittish. He was not happy and was very scared. We were one of the first ones for the judge to examine, and there were a lot of animals in the ring for the judge to look at; therefore, we had a long wait ahead before the winners were selected. It was going to feel like an eternity for this poor little guy.

While we waited for all to be examined, I sent calm energy through the lead line. I did my deep breathing while picturing that calm breath going down the line to this little alpaca. I was watching what the judge was doing as I did my breathing since I could feel what this little alpaca was doing from our connection through the lead-rope. I could feel him becoming calmer as the lead-rope tension eased. I looked down, and this little alpaca that had been so scared and skittish had placed his head on his sister's back and was sound asleep! Breathing really does calm you and your animal, especially in a very stressful situation.

Even if people go through all the various techniques and find they cannot do them, the one thing everyone can do is breathe. If we are mindful of our breathing, you will connect with your animal. Even if you don't hear them, they hear you and they feel your calmness when you breathe fully. What is nice is that it doesn't cost you a dime either! No fancy equipment, no high-tech gizmos needed. All you have to do is remember. It's as easy as breathing 1, 2, 3, 4!

Step 2: Observe Like a Field Scientist

Previously, I told the story of Miss Marple and observing how she didn't feel well. I know what normal behavior is for all my animals. Each animal has its own personality and way of doing things. They also share many common traits. Each species has their instincts, too. Getting to know your animal and their basic instincts is very valuable in communicating with them.

When I work with a client, helping with a pet that has behavioral issues, we spend some time discussing what the undesirable behavior looks like. I ask the owner to describe not just what the behavior is but also does it happen all the time? Are there times it is worse or certain times when it occurs and not others? I look for clues to see if there is a trigger that leads to that behavior. Many times, there is indeed a trigger, but the client hasn't been aware or seen it until we go back and walk through the various scenes. Often, the clients themselves will have "gut" feelings about the trigger but they haven't had confidence in their intuition to feel it was a valid idea.

I worked with one person who rescued a dog. With many rescue animals, we don't have much or any knowledge of their previous experiences. All too often, the rescue animal's history is not pleasant. In this case, the dog was very fearful. It ran away several times within the first days of being rescued. Luckily, he was found and brought back to his new owner. She was petrified for him but didn't know how to work with him, and she naturally had more anxiety knowing he could jump the fence.

Imagine being a rescued animal from a home that may have been an unpleasant and a fearful place. Perhaps this has been your only experience with humans. You are removed from that place and put into a new environment that is foreign, and you are picking up from a human a lot of anxiety and fear. You will recognize that emotion real well, wouldn't you! You'll lock on that like a radar. But, you may not be able to discern if that fear comes from a place of caring about your well-being or that you might hurt yourself. That may not have been your experience with humans thus far.

I worked on the breathing technique with the owner of this rescue dog and talked about managing her own anxiety. Although it was really hard for her to control her anxiety and worry over this dog running away, she managed it with this breathing technique. She said when she did that, the dog stopped trying to run away. She could point to the house, and he'd run inside. If she saw something that might upset him and produce his fearful state, she'd breathe and point to the house. That became their habit. He didn't have good recall and he didn't trust her yet enough to come to her, but he had a spot in the house where he felt safe. He was beginning to listen to her, and what he was hearing from her was that she was saying there is nothing to be afraid of.

Using observations, processing them, and writing them down often provide insights to your intuitive voice. I will have people write a paragraph of an event or observation with their animal, and I will tell them to use metaphors and adjectives to describe it to me. Using metaphors to describe the observation often gives us the language we need to gain insight to our intuitive abilities. Our intuition doesn't come with neon signs saying, "this is an intuitive hit!" Well not too often at least. We have these hits all the time, but because they are so subtle, we blow right past them and we wind up not giving them a second's thought. It isn't until they do become that neon sign that we pay attention to them. And many times, we never get to the point that they are so obvious that we can't deny the experience. We have to train ourselves to listen and tune into subtle, intuitive language. What is even trickier about intuitive language is that we each can have a different language. It is like we each have our own translator in understanding our intuition. Finding your own means of interpreting your intuition is part of the challenge.

I'll get into what I mean about your own intuitive language in Step 4 (page 32), when we discuss the various types of intuition. But the first task is training yourself to become an observer. I highly recommend starting a little journal of some sort. These observations and the language you use to describe them are keys to opening up to your intuitive abilities. To get to know your intuition and open up to it, begin with writing your basic observations. They may not be intuitive yet, but just observing behavior in your animal is a good starting point.

I worked with a couple who had rescued a cat. They had him just a couple of weeks and knew he had a really rough start in life. He was about eight years old and had a lot of baggage, but they wanted him because they knew he'd be hard to adopt out, being that he was older and having all his behavioral baggage. We discussed the behavior they were seeing that was obviously stress related. He was over eating, always hungry, and very insistent getting more food, his tail constantly moved, he slept for only short periods of time, and he wanted to be petted nonstop. He'd get upset if you stopped, to the point of biting.

I had them describe each of these behaviors many times over and was able to tie together that his background of neglect and not getting the attention was now resulting in this obsessive behavior of needing food and to be petted. Both behaviors came from that same place of being so deprived. I was able to do several emotional releases on him by removing many trapped emotions. As I did those releases, this lovely cat fell sound asleep. This was a behavior they said never happened when someone new was there. He was too hyper-vigilant, and they also said, he would never leave a new person alone because he wanted to be petted by them nonstop. Yet he let me do just a few pats, and then he hopped on a chair. As soon as I started to do my intuitive work on him, he fell sound asleep.

When I was done and we were talking a bit more about suggestions in working with this cat, he woke up and hopped off his chair. He walked to their slider window to look outside to their backyard. All of us noticed that his tail was perfectly calm and in a relaxed position. I was told it was the first time they had seen him stand with his tail perfectly still. He was much calmer than they had ever seen him.

Observations are important when our animals don't speak our language and even if we *do* know how to communicate intuitively with them, having a starting point and understanding of their behavior gives us clues to know how to connect with them intuitively. These body and behavioral language cues provide us with important information. They give us that starting point like on a game board, and we have a place to begin connecting with our pets as we get into the next steps of this book. But if we do not recognize their behaviors, both normal and abnormal, then we haven't even begun to listen to them. Even with this cat and his new owners, we didn't really need to know his background. They had a mere two weeks with him, and they were able to notice many things about him that gave us insights to helping him adjust and trust his new environment and people much faster. Observations are vital. They are an initial step that really can't be skipped when communicating with animals.

I've worked with animals in nature where there is no human to provide me with any insights or background about the animals. All I have is their behavior to observe in the moment. Even in that brief amount of time, I can still observe differences in behavior in them and subtle communication. In my book, *Alpacas Don't Do That*, I shared several experiences I had with various zoo animals and a couple of ducks. In many ways, practicing with animals found in nature right around your environment can help hone your intuition and build your confidence. Working with animals that are not your own, and especially ones like a bird sitting on a fence post or in your yard, can be really powerful and educational experiences.

Step 2's Five-Day Observation Writing Exercises

I've mentioned that writing or journaling is very helpful, but many people have a hard time starting or knowing what to write about. Here is an easy exercise to get you started. For five days, write a journal of your observations of your animal. I'll help give you ideas for those five days, but if you come up with your own ideas, go for it!

Day One: Think about a fun or cute behavior your pet does. Write and describe that cute behavior. When does it happen? Is there a specific time? A special place they do this cute thing? Does it remind you of any metaphors? Describe it as fully as you can. Perhaps include how it makes you feel, too.

You don't have to write pages and pages worth of descriptions. It can be a paragraph or two, but try to capture the behavior so someone who doesn't know your pet can visualize what this cute thing looks like.

Day Two: Write about your animal's habits at feeding time. Are they excited? Does it remind you that it is meal-time? Observe it for that day's meal and write about it. Is that what it does every time or was something different at this meal-time? Again, try to describe it as fully as you can.

Here is an example of writing a little comment or observation: *My collie, Fawkes, runs around the house as soon as I start to prepare meals. In my kitchen, where I feed her, you can make a full circle going around through my laundry room, to the living room, to the dining room, back to the kitchen. As soon as I start meals, she trots counter-clockwise and only counter-clockwise, making laps. As she passes me, she says woof-woof with her tail erect and fluffed out so full. She continues on with laps until the meals are fully prepped, and then she waits until I put her bowl in her spot. Her laps always make me want to sing, "She'll be coming around the mountain," and I often do. I can feel the joy coming from her that infects me, making my dogs' meal preparation not a chore but something we all look forward to.*

Day 3: Is there an undesirable behavior or habit your animal does? What is it and describe that fully. Have you seen that habit today? Does it happen regularly? Are there triggers that set it off? How do you react when it happens?

Day 4: Notice your pet sleeping or napping. Where are those places? Does he or she have a favorite position to sleep? Describe that favorite position. While you were observing your pet, were they in a favorite position or in a different one? What is its normal position and do you ever see he or she sleeping in an odd position? Does he or she have a special spot they sleep in the house, barn, yard? Describing sleeping patterns is very useful, especially with geriatric animals. How they sleep can sometimes tell you if they are feeling arthritic pain or other discomforts. Knowing what is normal can help you be more aware since animals are very good at hiding when they hurt, but you might notice subtle signals as they sleep.

Day 5: Does your pet have a favorite activity? Describe it. Does he or she play with toys, love to go for walks or go riding with you, or does it enjoy being brushed, hosed down? Describe how he or she behaves during the favorite activity. What is its body doing, and look like? If it has a tail, what position is the tail as it enjoys this activity? How about ears - what are its ears doing? What sounds do it make? Try to notice its body language. What are its eyes doing? Describe the feeling you have as you observe your pet. What is its connection to you or others as your pet does this activity?

I chose five days to get you started, but I really encourage you to keep going. It doesn't have to be every day. But try to jot down notes in a little journal. As you open up to your intuitive animal communication more and more, writing things down will help you notice very subtle trends and your growth that you would perhaps miss otherwise. It also trains you to observe more details as you continue journaling. You'll begin to notice more and more subtle signals, trends, habits, and triggers as you practice the art of journaling and note-taking. It also helps you stay focused and manage your brain's clutter.

Step 3 Check In and Check Out

In Step 1, I discussed the importance of breathing fully. Did you remember to do your breathing as you did your observing during Step 2 exercises? When we concentrate on one step, we often totally forget about the other. As soon as we start observing, we forget to do the full breaths. Both are easy things to do, but as we keep adding to the techniques, it takes a bit more concentration. The good news is that when you practice, these things become more second nature; it becomes easier to just breathe fully while staying focused on observing your animal(s). When I recommend doing the exercises in this book, I do so to help you get into the habit of doing them so you don't have to concentrate on them. In Step 3 of animal communication, we will work on multi-tasking and learning to observe ourselves at the same time we observe our animals. I call this chapter "Check In and Check Out" because we must remember to check in with ourselves as we check out our animals. Our animals can communicate with us in many different ways, and how we "hear" them can be very different than the two of us having a verbal conversation. To be able to translate the information you are receiving from your animal, you must know how you are doing before you get started. You need a baseline of how you are. Are you feeling pain? What emotional state are you in? If you don't check in on yourself, you may think that what you are experiencing is your own issue and it is easy to miss the animal reaching out to you with intuitive information.

If you recall, I suggest taking deep breaths or using the four-count breathing technique before you start working with an animal. During your breaths is the perfect time to do your "check in" of yourself. As you feel the breath coming into your lungs, act like a small body scan and start from your head and work your way down to see if you notice anything. Do you have a headache or stuffy nose? Are you smelling anything in the area? As you scan down your body, notice if anything else feels amiss or is going on in your environment. Is there any sound?

Like doing any kind of work, knowing where you are beginning is important information. Being aware of your own starting point will help you realize when something different is happening that just might be an intuitive hit. It is too easy to call something a coincidence or not even notice it if you don't do this check-in piece. I will do these check-ins throughout my communication with an animal. And I remind myself to breathe throughout the time, too. Again, if you practice these steps, it comes naturally. But in the beginning, it takes concentration and focus. I chose and honed these techniques to teach others with because they are so simple to do. But as you will notice as you start combining them, the coordination starts feeling like you are patting your head, chewing gum, and hopping on one foot all at the same time!

I was teaching my class, and we were learning the sway technique, which you will read more about in Step 5 (page 38). I was teaching a class at an alpaca farm, but they had a llama there as well. The llama stepped forward as I was getting ready to demonstrate how to do the sway technique to communicate with animals. I observed the llama's body language, and her eyes were communicating something to me. I just knew she was the one that wanted to be the demonstrator. However, my intuition stopped me from proceeding.

I normally demonstrate the technique myself, then take a volunteer and walk them through the steps, and then the class gets to go out in the field with the alpacas and practice on them. But I could "feel" this llama wanting me to do something differently. I had the entire class standing there, and I changed my way of teaching based on what this llama was communicating to me. A different thought of how I could proceed was put into my head, and I trusted it.

I like to verify my intuitive hits so I asked the llama if she wanted me to work with her, and using the sway technique, my body swayed backwards indicating a no answer. The llama had been looking intently at me, but then she took her eyes off of me and looked intently at one student in particular after she told me I wasn't the one she wanted to work with. I asked the llama if she wanted to work with this woman? The sway technique gave me the answer of yes (my body swayed forward indicating yes). So I skipped my demo and went straight to walking through the technique with this student the llama had chosen. The student performed the sway technique successfully, which is what I was teaching them to do.

I was about to release the class to go practice on their own when the llama looked at me with that same intent look that made me change up my teaching format. I felt that we weren't done yet. I quickly tried to check in on myself to see what else I might do with this llama. I asked the woman if she felt anything when she was working with this llama. She thought about it and said she felt very connected to the llama.

"No, that wasn't it," said the llama. She was trying to tell me, but I was having a hard time interpreting what it was that we were still to learn. I asked the llama to please help me to understand better, and just as I asked her that, she wiggled her ears in such a funny way. I have never seen an alpaca or llama wiggle their ears separately and like they were twirling about like she did. But that was the clue I needed. I asked the student, "*Oh!* Did you hear anything when you worked with the llama?" Again, the woman was tentative and thought back, and she said, "Well, I heard her hum." I smiled and knew that was what this llama was helping this student with. Although the woman heard the llama hum, none of us standing right there heard the llama hum. This woman was picking up the hum intuitively! The llama knew this student's strongest sense was in the auditory area and was helping her become aware that sometimes she "heard" things that others did not and that they could be intuitive hits so she should be aware and open to receiving intuitive intuition that way. With that information explained, the llama walked away.

When I talk about checking in and checking out, it can be very easy to miss those subtle cues and communications. In the story of the llama helping me teach the sway technique at a workshop, you can see how easy it could have been for me to miss those signals she was giving me. When I first started communicating with animals, I would be lucky if I just recognized that the llama or other animal was attempting to communicate with me.

When I was trying to interpret and figure out what animals were trying to tell me, I was often lost. I knew they were making the effort and try as I might, I wasn't sure what they were communicating. But I kept trying and practicing, and I have gotten pretty good at it. However, even now, I am not always successful at translating what is going on. The point being, don't worry if you don't get it all on the first try. But do try as it is the only way to get better at it. I could have easily stuck to my lesson plans and not listened to the llama who was very intent in wanting to work with this particular woman. And, even though I did change my plans to work with the llama, I could have very easily missed her telling me that we weren't done yet. We would have missed that very magical moment of the llama wiggling her ears to give me a clue of how to guide this woman to her bigger intuitive moment. And if this woman wasn't listening to her own check in, she may not have realized she heard a hum. The reason to keep trying is that you can have these amazing experiences of connecting like this woman did with her lesson with the llama. Telling the story, it doesn't do justice to having been a part of the actual experience. When you have your own experiences, you will know exactly what I mean. These moments fill your heart and touch you in ways that many experiences in life do not.

Checking in with the animal by observing them and yourself simultaneously is a bit of a juggling act. Having worked on radars for years, I understand how much processing has to take place after you transmit and receive signals. You have to be able to filter out the noise that isn't important, focus in on the information that needs to be examined more carefully, and recognize the piece of information that is the jackpot of information. But to do so, you have to continuously scan yourself at the same time as being very observant of the animal you are working with.

It is very common when I work with people and they are first beginning to open up to their animal communication skills that they write and tell me these lengthy great and clever stories about what they believe their animal is experiencing and telling them. I will caution you on this. We humans *love* to project our own feelings onto our animals. These projections are how we'd feel if we were having that experience ourselves, but that doesn't mean that is what the animal is truly experiencing.

We are all guilty of doing this, including me! If you get a quick hit of an emotion or feeling, a simple thought, a picture, or something you experience in your body that wasn't there before, that is more likely the real communication sent to you from your animal. That llama wiggled her ears just as I was asking for more information to guide that student. It was a brief and unusual thing for her to do, and it happened at the moment I was asking for guidance. It was something simple to give me a cue that I should think about ears.

It took me way longer to tell the story. The actual intuitive hits I received from that llama were so subtle and brief. She had an intent look. I had a feeling or thought that I was to do something different. I didn't hear a voice telling me, "You need to stop how you are teaching and do it this other way." Just the look, then the feeling of doing something different, and then another look at this woman. The rest of the intuitive interpretation came quickly. But no long story and voice telling me what to do and how to do it. There is a point when you start trusting these hits and letting them guide you. That is sometimes the hardest part. I don't always know where these hits will lead, and I have to let go of my original plans.

I recall when I was just opening up to my intuition. Several times when I was driving some place, I suddenly found myself driving a different direction than I had planned. I'd have this internal argument with myself as I tried to get myself to go in the direction I originally intended, but the car would have what seemed like a mind of its own as it headed in this other direction. I just had to keep following that direction, and I didn't understand why until I arrived. Sometimes the car would take me back home, and just as I was putting the key in the door, my phone (land-line in those days!) was ringing and someone needed me.

Another time I slowed down suddenly and put more distance between me and the car in front, which was going so incredibly slow. I had what felt like a thought placed in my head that told me to put more space between us. Slowing was keeping me from being in an accident was the thought I had. That intuitive hit was very clear. I listened to it, and sure enough as I approached this intersection, a car turning onto the road I was on lost control and hit the car in front of me, bouncing off and missing me by inches. If I had not put that distance between us, I would have been hit. These weren't animal communications, but they do show you that these hits can come in different forms, and learning to trust them can be very valuable.

When you let go of the need to create the stories, it becomes more of a puzzle to solve than creating a big story. You get to piece together the fabric of information you are receiving and try to figure out what question to ask to help you understand what an animal is saying. It can be really hard to let go of these stories. They often make us feel better because they really are about us after all. The stories can come in handy for understanding yourself better, but realize that they really are about you and not about the animal.

So how is writing down your observations, using metaphors and all these descriptions, different from creating these stories? It can get confusing, to be sure. If it was really clear-cut, it would be easy and we'd all be talking to animals like we talk to one another! Using metaphors and descriptions in your observations, gives you insights to your intuitive language. It is about you and giving you clues about you and your abilities. When you are observing your animal for communication, try to become a non-biased observer. Simply notice what is going on with the animal and start differentiating what is your experience and what is your animal's experience. Information can become very muddy with intuition because it is so very subtle at times. Your radar will get more finely tuned and you will get more used to what I'm talking about with practice. The techniques are easy to learn to connect; the interpretation is more challenging.

It has been my experience that animals have a varied emotional intelligence; however, it is a more limited emotional language than most adult humans. Their intelligence and emotional IQ are more equivalent to what a child would have. They can have very intense emotions just as a child does; however, if you think of the word "*love*," how many definitions would you guess a child would have for *love*? They would most likely have way fewer definitions for love than adults would. Like humans, some animals are more complex and evolved than others, and that is true within their own species as well as across species. I've met some humans who are not very evolved emotionally either! When you first start communicating with animals, think of reading a picture book or a child's first book. The language in children's books is pretty basic and simple, or it may tell the story with just pictures. That is the level of communication you should be looking for when listening to your animals. In other words, you won't get a novel!

Step 3's Five-Day Checking In and Out Exercises

In the "Check In and Check Out" step, we are starting to integrate Steps 1 and 2. These steps are very simple when we think of them individually. However, when we try to do them together it is like jumping on one foot while patting your belly with one hand and the top of your head with the other all while chewing gum! Each one done by itself is simple and very doable, but they get a bit more challenging to think about when trying to do them all simultaneously. But really, it just takes practice.

Day 1: This exercise will take you two minutes to do. Look at your watch, clock, or phone for time, practice your breathing fully and check in on yourself. Is anything going on in your body worth noticing? Also get a feel of what two minutes feels like when you are just observing yourself. You may find your mind wandering and starting to think about the day's activities and other matters. If you do, go back and look at the time and focus on your breathing. Picture the oxygen coursing through your body. Try to stay focused on you and your breath for two minutes. This is the check-in part. I recommend doing a little journaling after each exercise, so take a few minutes to do that.

Day 2: Spend two minutes doing your breathing and watching the time. Repeat the check-in phase as you did on Day 1. After your two minutes are complete, observe your pet/companion animal. Try not to look at your watch. See if you can get close to the two minutes without looking at your watch. How much time really elapsed when you thought the two minutes were up? Write in your journal what you experienced putting the two steps together? Did your animal do anything different? How did you feel? Write down things you noticed in both you and your pet.

Day 3: Spend two minutes breathing, two minutes observing your animal, as you did for Day 2 and now just sit or stand near your animal and just try to listen. Go back and forth between listening to you and listening to your animal and thinking about your breathing. If it helps, do it in intervals, for example, 20 seconds breathing, 20 seconds listening to yourself, 20 seconds observing and listening to your animal. Your animal may get up and walk away. If so, listen to it and end the session. They are concentrating on listening to you, too, and get tired as well. If you can do this for five minutes, you have spent a good, long session with them. Think about how long it takes to read a picture book to a child. That is about the time spent doing this exercise.

Day 4: Do the breathing exercise and don't look at your watch. Concentrate on your breathing and not letting your mind wander. When you feel you have done it long enough and are ready to break free of the focus and breathing, check your watch. How much time passed? Was it close to two minutes? Was it more or less? Did it feel like a long time, or did more time pass than you thought? Journal on how it felt. Was it easier to keep your mind focused? Harder? Did you find your body relaxed with the breathing?

Day 5: Begin with your breathing again, spending as much time as you need to check in and feel relaxed. Observe your animal again. Picture sending each of your breaths to your animal as if you are helping it relax, too. Do the four-count breaths, but picture and visualize it not just going into your body but also into its. If you have an animal that doesn't mind you touching them, place your hand on them and do your breathing. Don't try to pet; just give a light touch and focus on your breathing. Try not to force them to stay. If they wish to move, let them. If they walk away, continue your breathing and just observe. What is happening with them? Also check in with yourself. Are you breathing too? Are you able to continue your focus of breathing automatically? Or do you forget and need to remind yourself? Spend about the time you would take reading a children's book to do this exercise with your pet, and then journal what happened. Did you experience anything that you thought might be an intuitive hit? Did you feel anything different? Did you see, smell, taste, or hear anything unusual?

Step 4: Making Sense of It

In grade school, we are taught about our five senses: sight, hearing, taste, touch, and smell. Each of these senses also has a complimentary intuitive sense, plus there are a few more intuitive senses. In Step 4, we will be examining these intuitive senses. Most of us have heard about clairvoyance, the ability to see objects or actions beyond the normal range of vision. Psychic and intuitive ability are often interchanged as having the same meaning. I, personally, use intuitive more than psychic and see myself as more intuitive. Some can see into the future. I have had those experiences, but it is not my psychic strength. Some can see spirits and communicate with those that have passed. I have some experience doing that, and it is a psychic skill that I'm beginning to practice and hone, but it is not my specialty. Until recently, I had only a sense of my parents coming to visit, using smell to identify they were near. I'd suddenly smell pipe tobacco which my dad always smoked, and since my mom baked, the smell of banana bread was what she used to let me know she was near. I never bake or rarely do and never banana bread so if my house suddenly smells of banana bread, I know she has come to say hello.

Most psychics that I've seen on the television are mediums who can communicate with and receive messages from those who have passed. But again that isn't my gift. My intuitive strength is the ability to sense emotions. I consider myself an empath. I will quite often feel someone's pain or illness in my body, and that gives me clues to where energy should be released and healing energy sent. I am very honed into the emotions of animals and people. I can sense what emotions are related to those illnesses and can work on releasing those trapped emotions that can wreak havoc on our bodies, minds, and spirits. With animals, it is often trapped emotions that cause many behavioral, as well as physical, issues. I often say, we store our issues in our tissues. How that happens is for another book. However, being an empath is just another type of intuitive or psychic ability.

As I've described in the earlier steps, learning to translate the information received is the most challenging part of communicating with animals. Radars have several main components. There is the transmitter, which sends a signal into the environment, hits an object, and bounces back. That information is then received, and that signal is then processed in another device. This device performs the signal analysis that determines if the information received back matches whatever information that particular radar is looking for. A weather radar is looking for information like clouds and rain but doesn't care about airplanes that might be in the sky, too. A military radar, might be more concerned about those airplanes but not about the clouds, so it has filters that say "no, I don't want to display or take info on clouds, but I do want to let through info on airplanes."

When we develop our personal processor that analyzes the information we receive from animals, we first learn to determine whether this information is from ourselves or from the environment or is it from the animal? How we receive that information may come differently to each of us. I receive an animal communication most often as an emotion or physical difference in my body. I will feel a thought placed in my head. Some, like my student in the class that the llama worked with, may hear things. Some may see auras, and the colors can tell them what emotional state someone is having. I had one student who saw vibrations coming off of animals and people. She could see where the distortions were from illnesses or as results of emotional distress. She'd describe what she was seeing, but I couldn't see any of it. I can feel the vibration coming off of an animal and tell where the blockage is by feeling it. But I can't see it like this one student could. Others may smell things. I rarely smell unless it is my parents coming to visit from beyond. So you can see there are lots of different ways we can receive information intuitively.

Again, I suggest you keep a journal of your odyssey in growing your intuition. The language you use can give clues to how you receive intuitive or psychic information. As I describe my own empathic ways, I use the word feel a *lot*. I feel pain; I feel emotions of others. The word *feel* is something we empaths will use a great deal. Someone who is more clairvoyant will use sight words to describe experiences. They may say, "I *saw* that person about to run the stop sign." Or, "I just had a *vision* of where to find that lost animal." Someone may see vibrations or a person's aura.

You may see colors. Some associate colors with emotions. I knew a gifted psychic that could look at a person and she'd see colors vibrating off the person. She could tell the emotional state of a person by what colors she saw emanating from them. We "feel blue" means we are sad, we are "green with envy," we are "red with anger," and we are "yellow cowards," and so on. Others may hear things. They will use words associated with hearing, ie "a little birdie told me, and that was how I knew something was going to happen." My hearing is very sensitive at low and really high frequencies. On countless occasions as I walked the beach or drove along the coast, my head would turn and my eyes would automatically lock onto the exact location and time dolphins would pop up to get a breath of air. I believe my ears were picking up the ecolocation signals the dolphins were emitting. Some of those signals are out of the range of our normal hearing, however, I knew and felt I was "hearing," where the signals were coming from. Are you more sensitive to noises and sound? Think about what makes you sensitive when your five senses are concerned. Is there one that you are more sensitive to?

Just because someone may be really gifted with a discriminating sense of taste or smell, doesn't mean he or she can, as a "sensitive" person, see or hear just as well as he or she tastes or smells. My sense of smell and taste is much less evolved than my listening and sight. You may also have heard of different learning styles. Some of us are visual or auditory learners. There are kinesthetic learners as well as other kinds. We usually have one style with which we tend to learn better, but that doesn't mean that we can't learn using other methods. It just simply means one style is more effective and comfortable for learning. The same is true with our intuition.

The following are a brief description of some of the psychic senses. See if you resonate with one or more of the areas.

> **Clairvoyance:** Clear seeing or psychic vision abilities. You may use language like "I just had a vision of that car running the stop sign."
> **Clairaudience:** Clear or psychic hearing. You may use descriptive language like, "I heard a little bird whispering in my ear."

Clairsentience/Clairempathy: Clear or psychic feeling or sensing. You will find yourself using the word *"feel"* to describe your experiences, for example, "I just had a feeling that person was going to run the light."

Clairgustance/Clairambience: Psychic taste ability. You may find associating your intuitive experience with flavors.

Clairalience/Clairscent - Psychic smelling. I smell my mom baking banana bread when her spirit visits.

Clairtangency: Clear touching or psychometry. This is when you touch an object and receive information through the palms of your hands.

When I was first opening up to my intuitive abilities, it had to be very "loud" for me to recognize that it was an intuitive hit. Being an empath, I strongly felt people's discomfort in my body. It was not comfortable at all. If someone had a bad headache, suddenly I had a migraine, but as soon as they passed out of my energy field, it was instantly gone. I'd experience a severe pain in some part of my body so that I'd notice it, and then it would be suddenly gone.

On this one occasion, I was in an office supply store when this woman walked past me. I suddenly felt very queasy and light-headed. I thought, *"Uh oh, I must be coming down with a bug"*, but then this woman walked away from me and I felt fine again. My queasiness passed as fast as it came on. I continued my shopping when our paths crossed again and my queasy feeling returned. This repeated several times, and I thought, "*Maybe it isn't me.*" So I asked myself if this queasiness was mine. Yes or no? And I got "*no!*" Then I asked if there was something I should do about it. Did this woman need my assistance? I got the answer "*no,*" again. Since it wasn't mine and there was nothing I could do to help, I asked that this queasiness sense please leave my body. It did, and I stopped feeling queasy immediately, even when I was near this woman.

It was not comfortable having anothers pain in my body, but as I practiced asking myself if it was my feeling or someone else's and if I needed to do something about it, I honed this intuitive skill. Now when I feel other's emotions or pain, it is very muted. I have become more tuned into learning the difference and noticing the intuitive hit at a much lower volume. I use these psychic feelings to guide me in helping others. I must admit, during those earlier times of my intuitive development, it wasn't always pleasant. It was sometimes a tad scary. I sought out psychics with more experience and asked their advice in dealing with these uncomfortable feelings, and their advice helped tremendously.

As I began experiencing more intuition and recognizing that it was intuition, I didn't always understand what was being communicated to me. I could "feel" something happening. My hands would vibrate. I'd feel a pressure pushing against my forehead where the third eye is located. I could tell something was being placed in my head, some information, yet I couldn't provide any language for it.

What I believe happens when our intuition is being exercised is that those areas in our brain are being opened up and worked. These areas most likely have been dormant for a long time or haven't been used at all. As they are being dusted off and starting to be used, there usually isn't an instant connection to the verbal centers in our brain. It can take more practice and work to create those paths. I can feel that vibration or sense that something intuitively is happening, but I can't describe it yet.

I may experience something many times before I can finally put words to it. Or in the beginning when I was just starting to open up to my own intuition, I'd find books and read about how others' intuition worked and their language would make sense. They could describe what I was experiencing, and that language provided me with the verbal means to describe my intuition. For a handful of people, it is like a light switch, and they just suddenly know their intuition and have the language for it, but for most of us, it takes time to learn our own intuitive language. Personally, I think that is what makes this intuitive work so very interesting and rather neat. It is our own language that we have to learn to listen to. Our own voice, our own way of hearing and experiencing our intuition. There are developmental patterns and ways of helping you understand your own language. And someone like me who has a lot of experience with my own intuition and in helping others can help guide you in determining your own language. But it is *your* language.

What I've tried to convey in all these steps and techniques is to be patient with yourself. Keep trying. Stay open and practice. These techniques work, and you can learn. It just takes time and learning to trust yourself and the information provided. I can quite often help people tap into their animals our first session. But when I ask how they did between sessions, they have no confidence that it worked. They will often tell me they couldn't do it. I know they can because they did it!

One individual told me she could never do this intuitive work. She was adamant that she had no psychic abilities. She intuitively taps into her dogs all the time now! I bet the first time you were presented some math problems, you probably didn't know how to solve them. You didn't know what 2+2 was until you learned it. Now it is automatic, and you can do it without thinking. We have to start somewhere. Just because we are adults, we think we should know something right away. But if you are learning something you have never done before or it has been a very long time since using that information, it might take you a little while to figure it out. Not too many of us can pick up *War and Peace* in Russian and read it in its native language. We'd have to study Russian for awhile before we could read it in its original form. Be patient with yourself. Take classes; practice it with your animals, and with animals that you encounter. Ask your friends if you can practice with their pets. It is such a wonderful experience to connect with animals. Practice and hone your language! It is a wonderful gift to give yourself.

Step 4's Exercises:

Exercise 1: Read your previous journal entries. Highlight, circle, make note of descriptive words and phrases. Do you use "*feel*" often? Do you describe your experience through sight and vision? How about hearing? Do you use words or phrases like, "A little bird told me," "I just saw what was going to happen before it did," "a thought was placed in my head," or "I felt a vibration in my hands." Phrases and words such as these give you a clue. You can go to the psychic definitions on pages 33 and 34 to see if you can determine which psychic sense you may have been using. You may use more than one of the senses, and animals may use more than one to communicate *to* you as well. Being aware of how each sense can connect with you can help you be aware when an intuitive communication is coming through.

Exercise 2: Repeat the breathing and observation methods with an animal. If you can find one that is not your own, that would be great practice. You can even try an animal you see in nature. Breathe as you observe this animal. Do your scan of yourself and take note of anything you may be feeling that is yours. As you breathe and observe the animal, are you noticing anything? Do your ears ring or buzz? Do you feel anything in your hands? Any other part of your body feel anything different than before you started observing? How about your vision? Do you see any auras around the animal? Some people can see a vibration emanating from another being. Do you see that? Do you smell or taste anything? Does a thought suddenly pop into your head? How is the animal reacting to you? Is it watching? Did it stop what it was doing and act like it was listening? After you are done, write down what you experienced and notice the language you use. What sort of descriptive words do you use? Are they giving you any clues to what type of intuition you were using?

Is it important you know what intuitive sense you mostly use? It is helpful so that you can listen to that area more. However, if you don't know or are not sure, don't worry about it. Just stay open and scan yourself all the time anyway.

I was working with a dog with a behavioral issue. He told me that he smelled something that triggered his behavior. My nose is not one to discriminate smells at all. I am not one of those who can tell what ingredients are put into food like some folks can. I can determine maybe some stronger scents, but I can't define many odors. However, this dog was using smell to communicate to me. It is logical that animals would use scent to communicate intuitively since they have excellent scent skills. They greet each other by smelling each other's tushes! They can tell all sorts of things by smell that we cannot. So just because that isn't my strongest intuitive communication ability, I shouldn't write it off. It is important I am aware of information coming to me through all my senses. Most information comes through my strongest intuitive senses but I still receive with all my senses. It isn't vital that you know what intuitive strength is yours. It simply is helpful to understand that there are many ways of intuitive communication. You may recognize in yourself which is your way.

Step 5: Let's Talk — Using the Sway Muscle Test to Communicate with Your Animal

You've been very patient. The first four steps have been about listening and preparing you for connecting more deeply with your animal. Now, you finally get to actually do some talking with your animals! Hurray! Your patience will pay off. Doing all the lead up work of breathing and observing animals will do more to help you be successful in communicating with them. Doing those initial steps aid in gaining the trust of the animal you are trying to connect with. It demonstrates to the animal that you are willing to listen to them. After all, don't we all really want to be heard? Our animals are no different.

If you haven't watched my video showing the Sway Muscle Test to communicate with animals, or if you want a refresher, please take the time now to do so. Here is the link: https://www.youtube.com/watch?v=F522hPu8YUQ&feature=youtu.be

There are many ways of doing muscle testing. If the sway is not working for you, then you may want to try some of the other techniques to see which is most comfortable for you. I personally prefer the sway, and I am most accurate using it, but use the technique that is most comfortable for you. YouTube and Google are great resources for finding out more about these other techniques, and there are even some books written on the subject. But for this book, I will focus on the sway test.

The key to muscle testing and communicating with animals is learning to ask simple yes and no questions. There is an art to asking them. Open-ended questions do not work for this technique, and you won't get a long answer nor a response to a complex question. I will demonstrate in a moment what I mean by simple yes and no questions. I know I talk about practicing a lot, but that is what it takes. The technique is simple. How quickly you gain confidence and get the feel of how to ask questions is at your own pace and through your own path of learning.

Remember, keep your sessions short. Think of the time it takes to read a children's picture book. That is about the length of time you want to keep your sessions because your animal has the attention span of about that level and length of time. Plus, it takes both you and your animal considerable energy to keep that level of listening concentration going. You risk getting some false answers if you ask a lot of questions! Go ahead and write the questions down you want to ask your animals so you don't forget but do your asking and work in short intervals.

Before you begin talking with your animal, take several deep breaths. Always begin with a deep breath. Think of breathing as dialing the phone number when you want to call someone. You can't just pick up the phone and start talking to someone (at least our technology isn't at that point yet!). The number has to be dialed. Breathing is the phone number. If you are having a hard time getting your muscle testing working, do more breathing. Getting your body relaxed and open to receive is key to muscle testing. You will be listening to your own subconscious and your animal's. Your full breathing accomplishes two things. 1) It keeps you open and ready to receive information, and 2) it prepares your animal to want to listen to you. If you are stressed or angry, why would the animal want to listen to you? You will have much better success if your energy is pleasant to be around and breathing accomplishes that.

Stand with your feet about shoulder-length apart and make sure your knees are *not* locked. You will cut energy flow if you lock your knees. If you aren't getting the sway to work, check in: Are my knees locked? Am I breathing fully? If you feel tense, it is very hard to get your intuition flowing. Take as many deep breaths as you need to feel your body, especially your shoulders, neck, and legs, relax.

How the sway works is very easy. The subconscious is like a super computer, and it knows everything and won't lie to you. Your body will naturally move forward if the answer is true, or yes. If the answer is negative or false, your body moves backwards. Your body also moves forward when you think of positive thoughts and energy. It wants to move towards that positivity. The opposite is true. If you are thinking negative thoughts, or if you are upset, or angry or had an altercation before you try the sway, your negativity will make your body sway backwards. And that is the reason why I tell folks to breathe, clear their energy, and think of positive thoughts before they connect with animals.

Animals pick up whether you are in a positive frame of mind or a negative one. They will not want to be around the negative energy. They are very smart about that! When I go out and feed my alpacas in the evening, if I don't tend to my mood and I go out crabby, I invariably get kicked or spat on. (Fortunately, that is a rare occurrence!) If I go out in a happy mood, I receive kisses. The sway is a simple technique, and it works. Here is an example to show you how to apply this technique. Try this yourself so you can experience it.

To check to see if your sway is working, ask yourself your name. Think your name in your mind. Say and repeat, "My name is..." until you feel your body sway forward. Since that should be a true answer, your body will move forward. You will feel a slight pressure on the balls of your feet. Some feel the sway very strongly, and it nearly knocks them off their feet. With others it is very subtle. Check in and get used to listening to your feet. Try it a couple times stating, "My name is...."

Now to check for a false answer: Ask yourself a made up name. "My name is ..." and make up some ridiculous or totally false name. Listen to your feet. You should feel yourself sway backwards. Do you feel pressure on the heels of your feet? Try a couple of different false names. Then go back and forth between your real name and a false one. Get used to listening to your feet.

Next, try thinking of something very negative. Think about someone who made you mad. Recall something or someone that wasn't nice. Say the words *evil, hatred, mean.* Notice if you feel your body swaying backwards. Many feel the negative emotions very fast.

Shake off your negative thoughts, take several deep breaths, and think of something really positive. What do you love more than anything else? Picture a favorite place. Keep your mind on thinking such lovely, wonderful, glorious thoughts. Do you feel your body swaying forward? Our thoughts matter and emanate both good and bad energy out of us. Learning the sway test made me so much more conscious of my own thoughts. I choose to be more positive and keep my breathing flowing fully. It really has made me a much calmer and happier person doing this simple act.

If you have been able to do that, then you are ready to communicate with your animal. I start with its name. If you don't know its name (you talk to a critter in nature, say), then just describe or picture the animal in your mind. That animal will know you are trying to connect to it. I like to ask the animal permission to communicate with it. I will ask, the animal, "May I speak with you?" I wait for a sway. If I need to, I may ask a couple times if I'm not getting a yes or no response. The animal may think about it before giving you an answer. It probably is not used to a human talking to it that way!

When I was first learning, I was practicing intuitive communication with alpacas during shearing day. I was mentally telling them, what was going to happen to them. I thought to them saying that they'd be getting a haircut, nails trimmed, some pokes for medicines, and then they'd be done and back to their pastures to enjoy life again. As I started this mental mantra of activities, one alpaca whose turn was coming up turned to me and she literally did a triple take. She placed her nose right up against my face and sniffed me, and

I felt a thought placed in my head saying, "Hmm, I didn't know two-leggers could do that!" When we first begin communicating with animals, they are *not* used to us being able to communicate intuitively with them. They can be rather shocked so it could take a few tries of reaching out to them before they respond.

Once you have connected with the animal and if it says *yes* (your body moves forward), then, you can begin asking a few yes and no questions. If it is a dog, I may ask if I can pet it or I'll ask if I may take a step towards it. I do the same with a cat. I ask it a simple question. With a horse I may ask if it likes apples. Experiment with your questions. If you don't sway forward or backwards, that doesn't necessarily mean that your sway isn't working. It may mean that the answer is neither yes or no. It may mean you have to ask the question a little differently.

In the video I shared with you demonstrating this sway technique, you will see me asking my alpaca, Jamilah, if I can take a step towards her. My body moves forward with every *yes* answer she gives me. In this case, she never said *no* even when I asked if I could touch her. But when I receive a *no* answer, I respect it and do not step towards the animal. If the animal takes steps away from me, I respond by walking away from it as well. It demonstrates to the animal that you are listening to it and respecting its wishes.

It isn't unusual for animals to change their minds. They will maintain eye contact on you, and you can try asking again if you may take a step towards them. However, if I receive another *no* response, I stop and end the sessions with those animals. By listening to their body language and accepting that they don't want to engage, you will put so much into your trust account. Leaving on a respectful note is a real positive, and it will benefit you in the long run. Your goal is not to talk them into doing as you ask. The point is to be willing to listen and accept what they tell you.

You now have several tools to listen to your animal. You are listening to its body language and by using the Sway Muscle Test, you are listening to it intuitively. You are now observing it and yourself. You have to listen to its body language, your body as you sway, *and* any other intuitive hits you may get from the animal. The techniques are easy, but there is a *lot* happening. That is why I like using this simple muscle-test tool. Once you are practiced at using the sway technique, you will spend less time thinking about which direction you are swaying and be more tuned into your intuition. It does become easier with practice. Be patient in the beginning, and you will get proficient with the techniques.

When I first learned how to use my spinning wheel, it was very challenging. There was a lot to think about. I had to think about making my feet keep the pedals going, but not too fast and not too slow. I had to think about drafting the fiber so it would not be one big chunk, and I had to make sure the wheel was spinning in the correct direction. I think I'd have it working, then the fiber I was spinning would break and I'd have to start over. Each aspect took so much concentration. I persisted and practiced, and all of a sudden, the coordination came together. It was like a light switch, and I was spinning yarn! Now, I find it very zen like to spin because I don't have to think about each thing. My muscle memory knows what to do. I can just be in the moment of the art, and I don't have to think about what I'm doing. The same is true for using this muscle technique to connect intuitively with animals. In the beginning, it requires concentration to learn each piece. The more you do it, the more relaxed you get, the easier it gets, and you will notice your animal sending you more information.

As I was writing this book, one of my alpacas came up lame. As I worked with her, I thought, *this would be a great example of how to use all the techniques we learned in this book*. In this example about my alpaca Twister, I have underlined when I was using one of the five steps discussed in this book.

As I did my routine morning chores, I noticed out of the corner of my eye that Twister was limping. I walked over so I could see her better. I <u>observed</u> her barely putting any weight on her front leg. I took <u>several deep breaths to calm myself</u>. I always get anxious and upset when I see one of my animals not doing well. However, I know being anxious serves no one any good, and it makes it much more difficult to "hear" my intuition. Stress is nature's way of reducing our listening ability making it hard to hear others.

I took my deep breaths and calmed myself and observed how she was putting weight on that leg. I could tell it wasn't broken and by further observation, no swelling at her feet. She could bend her leg. It was my best guess she injured something in her shoulder area. I didn't believe this was an emergency and required immediate veterinary care. I always call my vet if I have any medical concerns, and doing energy work is not a replacement of calling a vet. *If you ever have an emergency with your pets, always call your vet. These techniques do not replace vet care.* But in this case, it was not an emergency and I could monitor her behavior.

I wanted to see if she had a thorn in her foot. I used the sway technique to ask if I could take a step closer to her. She said, "No!" When an animals are injured and vulnerable, they go into their instinct mode of trying to hide their injury and not wanting anyone near them as that is when they get eaten in the wild. Her instinct to keep me away was natural. I debated whether or not I should overrule her and catch her, but I decided to observe her for the time being.

I asked Twister if she'd let me perform some intuitive energy releases on her. I am able to release trapped balls of emotions or energy that get stuck in our bodies. I don't need to place my hands on the animal or person to do the energy releases. I can do it at a distance. One of my gifts is that I can do this energy work at a distance even when the animal or person is across the country or even on the other side of the world! But with an injured and vulnerable alpaca who already does not like being touched, being able to send the energy is a good thing.

I asked Twister in my mind if she would like me to do some energetic releases? She answered with a *yes* (My body swayed forward). After her energy releases, Twister was still putting minimal weight on that leg, but she was able to walk slightly better than before the energy work. She chose to join her herdmates and limped out to them. I continued to observe Twister the rest of the day.

The next morning I went out to check on Twister. She was already out with the herd, more relaxed and walking much better. I asked her intuitively if I could do more energy work on her. My body swayed forward (*yes*). I released several trapped balls of energy and then balanced her energy throughout her body. I used the sway technique and asked Twister to push my body backwards when she had received enough healing energy from me. I sent this balancing energy to Twister. While I was sending this healing, positive energy, I felt my body leaning forward and pressure on the balls of my feet. I stood in the pasture this way until I felt my body rock backwards when she had had enough. I kept observing her the entire time, and she was staring at me with direct eye contact the entire time I was communicating intuitively and performing the energy work on her. She was listening intently.

When I finished, I started to walk away, thinking we were done, but I noticed a very subtle sign. She didn't break her gaze from me like they typically do when they are usually done receiving energy work. My gut was telling me that Twister was still communicating with me even though I wasn't fully "hearing" her. I stopped and took a couple of deep breaths to try to "hear" what else she wanted me to do. The thought was put in my head that she wanted more releases. To confirm that was what she wanted, I asked her, "Do you want more releases?" My body swayed forward. I released those trapped energies, and as I released these balls of energy I felt an ache in my left elbow and numbness going down my fingers. It wasn't there before, and I knew that was a clue of what was hurting in Twister's body. As I released the last trapped energy on Twister, she turned her head away from me. She broke the communication with me, and I knew that we were done.

In this example, can you see how many ways I communicated with her? I used breathing, I used the sway technique, and I listen to my body when it gave me a clue of where the pain was. I listened to her body language to tell me when she wasn't done and when she was, and I confirmed that by using more Sway Muscle Tests and asking yes and no questions. A lot was going on in that example. Each session with Twister lasted less than 5 minutes which is about the time to read a children's picture book.

In this book, we aren't covering energy work, but you can see how many ways we can use this technique to get information from our animals. I use them to buy me time or when I don't have access to a vet, and I use them while working *with* the vet. Always consult your vet if you have any health issues or concerns with your animals.

The great value in helping animals that need to be seen by a vet, is that these techniques help calm them. As I mentioned previously, when animals are sick or injured, they feel not only the stress of the injury but their instinct to protect themselves. They don't understand that this strange vet's office where they can "hear" all sorts of stress coming from other animals is a safe place. It can make their anxiety even worse. Being able to tap into that level of trust you have earned with them and to communicate with them using your breathing techniques will help them stay calmer as they are examined.

I've been hired specifically to help calm animals at the vet's office. I've been told there was a noticeable difference in the animals that I helped during their vet visit. The animals were much less stressed, the doctor was able to examine them more thoroughly, and the owners were more relaxed, too.

I have to admit, nothing is harder than remembering to stay calm and breathe when our beloved animals are sick or hurt. It is way easier to help someone else's animal during these times. I don't have the emotional connection that you have with your loved ones so I can more easily remain calm. But when it is my own, it takes all my will power to park my stress so I can focus on helping my animals. I would much rather panic and freak out, but I know it isn't serving my animal. It takes *all* my skills and concentration to give my own animals what they need at these times. I like to teach people how to help their animals, but there are times when you need to call in the troops and get someone in who is not emotionally attached or has more expertise.

One of the biggest hurdles I help people with in learning this technique is building their confidence. I hear a lot of self-doubt and second guessing of the information they receive. When I help people in my classes and in one-on-one sessions, we move through those self-doubts much faster. Having someone that can guide you through those moments helps tremendously. I did a lot of second guessing myself and not trusting that what I was experiencing was real. I needed a lot of validation from animals before I accepted that it was really happening.

I remember talking with an eagle. I had no confidence yet that I could really communicate with animals, but I had the desire and thought, "Boy, wouldn't it be great if this was real!" I saw this eagle, and I wondered if I could work with him so I asked his permission and would he mind if I practiced communicating with him and doing some energy work. I told him I was just learning. It was the first time I have ever been scolded by an animal (but not the last time!). I had the thought put in my head that was very scolding in nature that said, "Nonsense! You already know how to do this." Despite being scolded, I still needed validation so I asked him to please raise his wings if he received my energy work.

As I worked on him energetically, I noticed an ache in one of my shoulders. I thought it was mine, but it had come on suddenly. I continued my energy work, and when I was done, the eagle raised one wing and looked intently at me with his piercing eyes. He cawed with the loudest, most magnificent caw I have ever heard from any kind of bird. It was amazing! It was then that I noticed that he had raised only one wing. The other wing had been amputated. Where the amputation was correlated to where my shoulder was aching. It validated my intuitive abilities as an empath *and* as one who communicates with animals.

Back then, when I was learning to communicate with animals, I felt very isolated. I didn't share what I experienced with very many people. I trusted only one or two individuals with my experiences. I didn't have an experienced animal communicator or intuitive energy worker I could seek out for mentoring. After I gained confidence and began working with a lot of animals, I decided on my own direction for using this gift. I knew that I wanted to help others learn and build their confidence and to not feel they had to do so in an isolated vacuum. There is someone out there who believes it is real, who knows it is real, and who can guide you in learning your own language of communicating with animals.

I like to use the metaphor of bridges. There are all types of bridges. There are major bridges like the Golden Gate and Brooklyn bridges, there are railway bridges, foot bridges, rope bridges, covered bridges, and so on. Each different type of bridge is like the different style of communication we may use, like verbal language, body language, or any of the intuitive languages we learned about in Step 4 (page 31). When working with animals, we can also include using the lead rope or reins as another form of communication.

The key thing to learn is that whatever type of bridge you use, it is a two-way communication. If we want to talk to someone on the other side of the bridge, we can possibly yell across the bridge to be heard, but that is probably not super effective. The great thing about bridges is that we can cross them! And the best way to get someone to hear you, is to cross over to their side of the bridge. We may want the individual to eventually cross to our side, but if we want them to join us, we have to go join them on their side first. If they are scared to cross over that bridge, it is even more important to join them on their side first. Escort them across. Help them build confidence and trust in you and the bridge.

Using your breath is a bridge. So is using the lead rope or using your words and emotions. It may seem like you are doing nothing when you are just breathing, but I guarantee that you are doing a very important and powerful thing. It is crossing over to animals' side of the bridge and connecting with them in a language that they understand even if you don't fully understand it yourself. Animals are great and generous teachers. We just have to show them we are willing to use languages they understand. They are patient with us, and they don't judge us when we don't get it right. They may walk away, but they won't make fun of us!

While we work to provide a safe environment for our animals to trust us, they too give us safe relationships to put ourselves out there when doing something that is perhaps uncomfortable because it is new to us. It can feel awkward and weird, and if we are practicing these skills with other humans who aren't as open minded, we might worry about how they may see us.

This level of communication is very intimate, and it can make you feel vulnerable. You are opening up to your innate abilities and intuition, and that can be a very sensitive area of your psyche. Animals take care of that vulnerability like no others. They are patient, let us make mistakes, and forgive us when we aren't perfect at communicating their way. Letting go of our pride and ego is part of allowing this intuitive communication to grow. Or rather, we get to let go of the unhealthy aspects of ego and pride and keep the healthy aspects.

After we get more confident in our abilities, we stop caring about what others say. When we worry how others perceive us, we are tapping into that unhealthy ego and pride. Having a deeper relationship with animals is real and valuable to us. And that can be the best gift of all in learning to communicate with animals. It makes us better humans.

About the Author

Cindy Myers owns and runs her own farm, Alpacas at Hum Sweet Hum in Oregon. She does Animal Communication services under the business name of Animal Listener. She also does energy work on human clients. She has her M.A. in Counseling Psychology with an emphasis in Depth Psychology from Pacifica Graduate Institute and has a B.S. in Aerospace Engineering from San Diego State. Cindy also has level II certification in Reiki and is a Healing Touch practitioner. She is also certified in TAGTEACH. She teaches workshops in Positive Reinforcement Techniques for training alpacas in addition to writing, spinning her alpaca's fiber, and caring for her alpaca herd, three dogs, and two cats. She is also the author of the book *Alpacas Don't Do That* and has had articles in numerous animal-related magazines. You can find out more about Cindy at her website, BeAnAnimalListener.com.

Using body language and breathing to gain trust of a baby alpaca

Observing your pet can provide useful information. Plus you can catch them being stinking cute!

I can feel vibration and heat coming off of Minnie in areas she had blocked energy.

Cindy, Dulcinea and Twister having a special moment together